Diet consisting solely of raw foods

Purify Your Eating Habits With a CleanJ Plant-BasedJ Healthful Approach

Elizabeth T. Mabry

Contents

Chapter One

Introduction

A raw food diet is one that consists mostly of uncooked, whole, plant-based foods that are ideally organic. Uncooked foods should account for three-quarters of a person's total caloric intake.

Typically, raw food accounts for 70 percent or more of a person's daily caloric intake. Fruits, vegetables, sea vegetables, nuts, seeds, sprouted grains, and legumes are all staples of the raw food diet. It is fine to gently heat food as long as the temperature does not rise over 118 degrees Fahrenheit.

While the majority of individuals who follow a raw food diet plan are vegan, some do consume raw animal products such as raw milk, cheese derived from raw milk, raw fish or meat, and raw eggs.

This cookbook will guide you through a clean, plant-based, wholesome approach to eating that will alter your health via the use of vegetables, fruits, nuts, and seeds, among other things. The foundations of a raw diet are covered in this cookbook, whether you are making a few changes to your weekday dinners or completely revamping your diet.

In this cookbook, you will find a thorough breakdown of the raw food diet for beginners, including defining the diet, explaining its benefits, listing foods to eat and those to avoid, providing suggestions for incorporating the diet into an existing meal plan, and describing how to obtain all of the nutrients you require.

Raw Food Recipes: There are over 500 recipes that are divided into categories such as dessert, breakfast, main dishes, soup and side dishes, salad and dressing.

Substitutes for Raw Foods: Refer to nut-free alternatives as well as substitute suggestions.

Preparation Time: 20 minutes || Total Time: 20 minutes Stuffed Avocados with Crunchy Asian Cabbage Slaw Preparation Time: 20 minutes This recipe is in the breakfast category and makes 4 servings.

Chapter Two

Raw Granola with Edible Blossoms

Ingredients

2-3 cups peeled, peeled and cubed yams

2 dozen pitted medjool dates

1 vanilla bean, 2 teaspoons cinnamon, 1 teaspoon sugar

2 tablespoons coconut butter and 1 teaspoon sea salt

3-cups of distilled water

1 heaping tablespoon of psyllium powder

1 pie crust with nuts and dates

a sprinkling of chopped walnuts, and a drizzle of raw honey

Instructions

Using an immersion blender or a food processor to blend the ingredients until smooth, add the water and process until it is completely smooth again.

Mix in the yams until they are completely blended.

Psyllium should be added after thoroughly mixing.

For a thicker consistency, set the mixture aside for 5 minutes.

Blend until the mixture is smooth once more if necessary.

Place the filling in the piecrust and top with slashed walnuts that have been treated with honey to make them more flavorful.Oats (whole) soaked overnight or at least 4 hours before cooking

raw almonds (I used honey-glazed almonds) 3 cup raw walnuts, chopped 12 cup raw sunflower seeds 3 cup raw almonds (I used honey-glazed almonds)

a 14 cup cup of raw pecans, cut tiny a 12 cup cup of raw honey (if feasible, get to know your grower; mine comes from a family member in Oregon)

1 / 4 cup Agave or Maple syrup (very optional)

1 tbsp. Ground Cinnamon (or to taste)

Himalayan Salt (Pink Himalayan) 1 teaspoon

Directions:

Crust made from scratch

1 cup shredded coconut (optional)

12 cup toasted pecans

1 cup toasted walnuts

Medjool dates (six Medjool dates) (or 12 soaked normal dates)

2 tablespoons Agave Syrup (optional)

1 / 4 teaspoon of salt

2 tablespoons melted Coconut Oil (optional) Recipe for Raw Food Caramel

2 cups of soaked dates - soak for a minimum of two hours, then drain well.

14 cup unprocessed honey

1 tablespoon Almond Butter (you may eliminate this if you can't locate it or if you can't find a raw form of it) Instead, use an additional spoonful of honey.)

Almond milk (two tablespoons) and one-fourth teaspoon salt

Strawberry Topping Recipe in Raw Form

400-500 g strawberries, cleaned and cut into quarters or halves.

2 teaspoons Agave Syrup Preparation Method

Preparing the raw receipt with the required timeframes requires soaking the dates for the caramel and foundation.

When you are ready to prepare the Raw Crust, place the nuts in a food processor and pulse until finely chopped. Continue to combine until a doughy, chunky mixture is produced by adding the remainder of the ingredients.

Place the mixture into oiled tart pans; alternatively, muffin tins may be used, or a big cake tin can be used to create one huge tart/flan.

Prior to filling, place the container in the freezer for 4 hours to set. DO NOT MISS THIS IMPORTANT STEP!

All of the caramel ingredients should be combined in a food processor and processed until completely smooth.

Pour the mixture into tins, molds, or whichever containers you're using. Gently arrange all of the strawberries into your circular tiers, finishing with a whole strawberry in the center for display purposes.

For the best results, pour the Agave Syrup in a basin in the sink filled with warm water approximately 20 minutes before you want to use it. Gently drizzle a splash of agave syrup over each one to bring out the color of the strawberries. Refrigerate for 3–6 hours before serving.

Amy's Pea and Cucumber Dip/Spread (recipe below)

Prepare your sprouting peas according per package directions.

a half cup of dry peas

Instructions

Place in a tub in a closet overnight after soaking in 1 cup water. The next morning, rinse and drain the tub.

Repeat this procedure for the following two days. They should have a little amount of money presently.

tails. Add 3″ sliced cucumber to the peas and mix well.

Nutritional yeast (around 1 teaspoon)

A few of fresh sage leaves or some mint would do the trick.

2 cloves of garlic, peeled and minced

1-2 tablespoons extra-virgin olive oil

Instructions

If you have access to a hand blender or a liquidizer, puree the mixture (in this case put cucumber and oil in first)

Season with sea salt and freshly ground black pepper to taste, then bake for 30 minutes at 350 degrees.

Raw Salted Blueberry Chocolate Tart is a dessert recipe type that is raw vegan in cuisine.

In a large mixing basin, gently combine all of the ingredients.

Distribute the mixture onto dehydrator sheets (I didn't use paper and nothing trickled through).

Dry until the mixture is crunchy/crisp.

Remove from dehydrator and season with more honey and cinnamon to taste; return to dehydrator until crispy and done!

I threw in a few edible blooms from my own garden (lavender petals, Bok Choy blossoms, borage, pansies and violas). You may always add extra dried fruit, nuts, seeds, spices, or anything else you want to this recipe.

Finish with homemade nut milk; I chose hemp milk, but any nut milk would do. 7. Take pleasure in and continue to consume your plants!

Tarts with strawberries and caramel preparation time: 10 minutes || total time: 10 minutes Cooking Style: Vegan Yields 3-4 servings

Ingredients

1 cup finely chopped red cabbage (I recommend using a mandolin)

1 cup finely chopped green cabbage

a third of a cup grated carrot (about 1 carrot)

1/2 cup finely sliced red onion

4 finely sliced green onions (optional)

1 tablespoon finely chopped fresh ginger 1 lime juice

2 tablespoons mirin

1 tablespoon of rice vinegar

1 tablespoon turbinado sugar (or brown sugar)

2 tablespoons of roasted sesame oil

2 avocados, half, with sesame seeds pitted on top

Instructions

In a medium-sized mixing bowl, combine the two cabbages, the carrot, the red onion, and the green onion.

In a small mixing bowl, combine the ginger, lime juice, mirin, rice vinegar, sugar, and sesame oil until well combined. Pour the dressing over the cabbage mixture and toss to incorporate.

Carefully scoop a hole into either side of the avocado. Fill the tortilla with the slaw and sprinkle with sesame seeds. Enjoy!

NOTES

Mini slices of avocado and a tablespoon of slaw may be placed on a rice cracker or sesame cracker to make a small appetizer version of this dish. Sesame seeds may be used as a garnish.

is a healthy snack option.

Time required for preparation: 10 minutes || Total time required: 10 minutes Vegan cuisine is available. This recipe yields 3-4 servings.

Chapter Three

The Crust's

Ingredients are as follows:

70 grams of hazelnut flour and 75 grams of almond flour are used.

2 tbsp. coconut oil (optional)

A teaspoon of sea salt and 2 tablespoons maple syrup

Filling: 1.5 cups dates, soaked overnight and drained, for the topping:

14 cup cashews (about)

14 cup warm water seeds from a fresh vanilla bean (about 12 seeds)

80 g 70% dark chocolate, melted (80 g total) For the icing on the cake:

1 cup of freshly picked blueberries

melted chocolate (30 grams) 30 grams chocolate

12 tbsp coconut oil or ghee (optional)

12 teaspoon coarse sea salt, kosher if available

Instructions

Combine the hazelnut flour, almond flour, coconut oil, maple syrup, and sea salt in a Cuisinart or blender until well combined.

Blend until everything is well-combined.

Make a ball out of the dough by removing it from the blender and rolling it with your hands.

Fill a tart pan equally with the mixture (mine is irregular at 8 inches wide, but you could use two 4.5-inch- wide tart pans).

Blend until creamy in consistency the following ingredients: drained dates, cashews, heated water, vanilla bean, and melted chocolate (it took me about 1 minute, total, stopping to scrape down the sides every 15 seconds or so).

Filling should be poured over the uncooked crust.

Distribute evenly.

Blueberries should be scattered on top, in no particular order.

Incorporate the remaining of the chocolate with the coconut oil or ghee, swirling well to properly combine the two ingredients together.

Spoon melted chocolate over your berry topping one little spoonful at a time, working quickly (I used two spoonfuls).

Using coarse salt, cover the surface.

Refrigerate until ready to serve.

DIET OF RAW FOODS

The raw food diet may trace its origins back to the late 1800s, when a doctor claimed to have treated his own case of jaundice by consuming raw apples in raw form. Since then, the diet has developed into its present form, with its popularity fluctuating between peaks and troughs. Sometimes individuals go from a vegetarian to a vegan diet, and then from a vegan to a raw diet.

A raw food diet consists mostly of unprocessed, entire, plant-based foods that are ideally organic in nature. Uncooked foods should account for three-quarters of a person's total caloric intake.

Typically, raw food accounts for 70 percent or more of a person's daily caloric intake. Fruits, vegetables, sea vegetables, nuts, seeds, sprouted grains, and legumes are all staples of the raw food diet. It is fine to gently heat food as long as the temperature does not rise over 118 degrees Fahrenheit.

While the majority of individuals who follow a raw food diet plan are vegan, some do consume raw animal products such as raw milk, cheese derived from raw milk, raw fish or meat, and raw eggs.

A raw food diet consists of ingesting fresh, nutrient-dense plant foods that have not been heated or processed in any way. When foods are cooked, they lose a significant amount of their key disease-preventing components.

A raw diet, on the other hand, provides you with a better degree of health and energy, slows the aging process, and aids in the healing process. Healthy raw foods should be the bulk of your diet, with harmful alternatives avoided at all costs. This will enhance your health and lower your chances of developing a degenerative condition. It is simple to begin living a more healthy lifestyle.

People who follow a raw food diet think that consuming a large percentage of raw foods makes them healthier. Some raw foodists are vegans, which means they do not eat any foods derived from animals. Others consume raw meat and raw animal products, which are considered to be a health risk.

The Raw Diet allows you to consume the following foods:

Foods that are easily identified as raw include fruits and vegetables that are picked fresh off the vine. It may be necessary to study labels and spend some time searching for raw ingredients such as nut butters, agave nectar, almond milk, olive oil, soy sauce, and chocolate if you're using other components.

It is not raw food if it has the phrases roasted, toasted, cooked, or baked in the title or on the packaging. The same cannot be said for canned goods.

Foods that are in compliance

Unprocessed meals that are as close to nature as possible

Nuts, seeds, and fruits that are grown organically

Beans and grains that have sprouted or germinated

Dishes that are made from scratch using fresh ingredients

Vegetables

Salads, smoothies, blended sauces, and soups may all benefit from the addition of veggies to their recipes. It is possible to pickle vegetables or make vegetable noodles out of them, as well. Frozen veggies that have been blanched or boiled before being frozen do not qualify as raw vegetables. Arame, dulse, kelp, wakami, and unroasted nori sheets are some of the sea vegetables to watch out for.

Fruits

A variety of fruits may be consumed in many forms, including whole, dried, dehydrated, and juiced. The term "raw" refers to uncooked fruit, such as frozen fruit. The raw food diet allows for the consumption of a variety of superfoods such as raw cacao powder, cacao nibs, carob powder, and goji berries among others.

Fruit and seeds such as almonds and sunflower seeds

Choose raw, organic nuts and seeds wherever possible. You may use them in smoothies, pesto, butters, non-dairy milk, cheeses, gravy, cream, and ice cream, among other applications. Raw chia or flax seed crackers may also be made in a dehydrator using the same method.

Grains

Whole grains such as millet, buckwheat groats, kamut, quinoa, oats, wheat germ, spelt, and wild rice are all permissible on the raw food diet, but they must be germinated or sprouted prior to consumption.

Beans and legumes are a kind of plant that is found in the legume family.

Following sprouting and soaking, certain raw beans (such as chickpeas and lentils) may be consumed, whilst others (such as kidney, soy, or fava beans) are deemed dangerous to consume.

Acai berries, raw coconut oil and butter (coldpressed, extra-virgin olive oil), chia seeds, raw flaxseed oil, and raw hemp seed oil are all excellent sources of raw fats.

Beverages

Beyond purified water, raw foodists consume barley grass juice, vegetable or fruit juice (freshly squeezed or frozen, unpasteurized), young coconut water, and wheatgrass juice, among other things. The use of caffeinated beverages is prohibited, thus black and green teas as well as coffee must be avoided throughout the diet. Due to the fact that the leaves are often heated during the production process, herbal tea (even when brewed with water heated to less than 118 degrees Fahrenheit) is not considered "raw."

Foods that have been fermented

When following a raw food diet, it is permissible to consume foods that are fermented. There are a variety of fermented foods available, such as coconut kefir or yogurt, kimchi, miso paste, and sauerkraut.

Flavorings such as herbs, spices, and sauces

When it comes to the raw food diet, table salt is not authorized; however, Himalayan and Celtic sea salts are, as are the following seasonings:

Cider vinegar made from apples

Liquefied Aminos with Cayenne Pepper by Basil Bragg

Chives

Choco, raw Cinnamon, ground Cumin, ground or seeds, and a variety of other ingredients

Curries

Root of the dill (ginger)

Nama shoyu is a Japanese word that means "name of the shoyu" or "name of the mountain" (raw soy sauce)

Raw Vinegars with Parsley, Vanilla, Vanilla Beans, and Vanilla Beans

Sweeteners Although most sweeteners are processed and hence not completely raw, the following are permissible: raw agave nectar, raw coconut nectar, raw honey, mesquite powder, stevia powder, date sugar, and yacon syrup. Sweeteners are not permitted in large quantities.

When following a raw diet, avoid the following foods:

Various individuals have varying ideas of what the raw food diet is and what it means for them. A portion of prepared food will be consumed by some, but no food will be consumed by others. Some consider it to be an extension of their personality and way of life. Others consider it only a matter of personal preference when it comes to their diets.

Foods that aren't in compliance

Foods cooked at a temperature greater than 118 degrees Fahrenheit processed foods, such as those that have been refined, pasteurized, or heated

Pesticide-treated foods are those that have been exposed to pesticides.

Caffeine

Olives: If you eat them uncooked, they are bitter. Olives, on the other hand, may be consumed fresh and sun-cured by a raw foodist. In addition to cooking olives, most olives are preserved by salting them before storing them in a container.

Salinity is measured in milligrams (mg).

Drinking alcohol (coffee, tea, and other beverages)

Pasta

cooking and chopping vegetables

An individual who practices raw food preparation does it in an unusual manner.

It is only permitted to use a dehydrator for heating purposes. Using this method, heated air is blown through the meal being prepared. At no point does the temperature rise over 116 degrees Fahrenheit, which is equivalent to 46 degrees Celsius. It is also acceptable for raw foodists to combine and cut their food.

We consume grain and bean seeds that have been soaked and sprouted rather than eating them in their natural state

To soak nuts, soak them in water, and dry some fruits

The juice or smoothie of several fruits and vegetables is popular.

Soaking and sprouting are two methods of growing food.

Raw beans, legumes, nuts, and seeds contain enzyme inhibitors, which are generally removed by heating, but are not destroyed when eaten raw. If you soak or sprout them, you may liberate the nutrients that are locked within.

It is necessary to soak the seeds in water for a specified period of time before they can germinate. However, some raw foodists believe that soaking cashews overnight is adequate and more convenient than the suggested germination durations, which range from two hours (for cashews) to one day. It's essential to start with dry, raw, and ideally organic seeds, beans, legumes, or nuts as a base for any recipe or snack.

Fill a glass jar half-full with rinsed legumes or seeds and store them in the fridge. Pour in enough filtered water to cover the ingredients at room temperature. Lie down in a warm place overnight (mung beans require a full 24 hours). Before using, thoroughly rinse the container.

Seeds, beans, and legumes may all be sprouted once they have been germinated. Place them in a container for sprouting once they have been drained during the last phase of the germination process. Allow them to cool to room temperature before serving. A sprout will emerge from the seed, bean, or legume once it has opened. Make sure to thoroughly rinse and drain the sprouting nuts or seeds. In the refrigerator, they may be kept for up to five days if placed in an airtight container.

Dehydrating

It is possible to replicate sun drying by gently heating foods in a dehydrator, which is a piece of equipment that is available for purchase. Dehydrators are containers containing heating components that allow food to be heated at low temperatures while being stored within the container. In the dehydrator, heated air is circulated through trays of food by means of a fan within the unit. With the use of a dehydrator, you may prepare a variety of foods such as raisins, dried tomatoes, kale chips, crackers, bread, croutons, and fruit leathers.

Preparation of Blended and Juiced Products

Smoothies, pesto, soup, and hummus may all be made by blending or chopping foods in a food processor or blender. You may also make juice out of vegetables and fruits.

Fermenting

Sauerkraut, raw coconut yogurt, raw macadamia nut cheese, and kimchi are all examples of fermented foods.

Modifications

Vegetarian, vegan, and gluten-free diets are all suitable with a raw food lifestyle. Preventing food-borne infections is made easier using cooking techniques (such as E.coli).

Pregnant women, children, elderly individuals, persons with compromised immune systems, and those suffering from medical illnesses are not encouraged to follow a raw food diet.

When it comes to the raw food diet, those with a history of eating disorders or those who are underweight should check with their healthcare professional first, since it is often quite low in calories.

2

There are several advantages to eating raw foods.

Vitamins included in raw fruit help to protect the body from the damaging effects of free radicals. Chronic disorders such as cancer and heart disease are exacerbated by free radicals in the body.

In case you're concerned about overindulging in carbs when you eat fruit, keep in mind that fruit is a simple carbohydrate, and the sugars in fruit are readily absorbed by cells and used as a power source.

You'll also receive a lot of fiber and antioxidants from entire fruit since you're eating it whole. In addition to adding protein to your breakfast, you'll want to include a serving of fresh fruit and some chopped nuts and seeds for healthy fats to round out your meal.

High concentrations of minerals such as iron, calcium, and magnesium are found in vegetables. These minerals are required by our bodies for a variety of metabolic processes, neuron function, and a slew of other critical functions.

It is a combination of several minerals that aids the body in maintaining regular health and functioning. Of course, veggies include a significant amount of antioxidants, so you'll want to incorporate a variety of fruits and vegetables in your raw food diet as well.

Consuming mostly uncooked meals, according to raw foodists, may help you lose weight.

Many novice raw food dieters may likely lose weight at initially due to the elimination of processed foods.

The raw foodists also think that by following a raw food diet, the body is better equipped to avoid and fight illness, particularly chronic disease.

Foods that are eaten raw have a higher concentration of some nutrients, such as water-soluble vitamins B and C, which are diminished or eliminated by cooking.

As a result of the presence of vital food enzymes in raw and live foods, they claim, These food enzymes are destroyed when the meal is heated over 116 degrees Fahrenheit (47 degrees Celsius).

Those who practice raw foodism believe that enzymes are essential to the survival of a meal. The precise combination of flavors and nutrients found in each item has been created by Mother Nature. These essential enzymes help us to thoroughly digest our meals without having to depend on our own digestive enzymes. They are essential for our health.

These enzymes, as well as vital vitamins and minerals, according to raw food advocates have been destroyed or altered by the cooking process. They claim that only "living" food is available in its natural state.

Those who believe that cooked meals take longer to digest clog the digestive system and arteries with fats, proteins, and carbs that have not yet been fully digested.

Raw food advocates claim that following a raw food diet will result in the following symptoms:

Increased physical activity

Skin that is clearer

digestion is more efficient

Obesity management

Decreased likelihood of getting heart and cardiovascular diseases.

a decrease in the risk of cardiovascular disease, cancer, obesity, and type 2 diabetes a

What to Keep on Hand for Raw Food Preparations

The health advantages of raw food may be enjoyed at any time of day or night with a little forethought and preparation. A list of raw items to have on hand can help you prepare meals in minutes:

A variety of fruits such as blueberries, oranges, bananas, and avocados are particularly versatile..

Seasonal veggies that are picked right out of the ground

Leafy greens such as kale, spinach, cabbage, and romaine lettuce are among the most nutritious foods available.

nuts and seeds that have been soaked in water

Wheat germ or buckwheat are gluten-free grains that have been sprouted or steamed to remove the gluten.

Lentils, peas, chickpeas, and beans are all legumes that may be sprouted or cooked.

Raw sauerkraut, miso, and raw yogurt are examples of probiotic-rich foods.

Being Well-Nutritioned While Following a Raw Food Lifestyle

What to consume when you first begin to convert to a raw food diet might be difficult to discern. Be adventurous and try new foods, but be sure to follow these dietary guidelines to ensure that you are getting the appropriate nutrients you require:

Consume a broad range of fruits and vegetables that are fresh, ripe, uncooked, and organic in origin.

All of the hues of the rainbow should be consumed to get a complete range of nutrients.

Make green vegetables, which are high in nutrients and fiber, the bulk of your meal plan.

Keep raw nuts and seeds in moderation by consuming a range of different types.

Include foods high in omega-3 fatty acids in your diet.

Fried meals, saturated fats, and oils should be avoided to the greatest extent possible.

Nuts, seeds, and legumes should be soaked and sprouted prior to consumption.

To reduce chemical residues, go for organic products wherever feasible.

Make meat and dairy items a part of your diet only in moderation or completely eliminated.

Restrict the intake of sugary foods and concentrated sweeteners such as white sugar, corn syrup, evaporated cane sugar, soda, candy, and desserts prepared with sugar, as well as other high-calorie foods and beverages.

Salt should be used only in moderation.

Grain alternatives that are gluten-free include quinoa, millet, amaranth, and buckwheat.

B12 should be taken as a supplement.

If you don't receive enough sunlight, you might consider taking a vitamin D supplement.

On a raw food diet, there are several surprising natural foods to avoid.

Whenever you hear the phrase "raw food diet," you're probably thinking of meals that aren't fried, roasted, baked, or grilled. And you're probably accurate in thinking that.. Some raw foodists avoid highly processed meals as well as those that are excessively sweet or salty or that are fatty or greasy in any way. It is not the whole tale, though, as the next paragraph explains.

More meals that may look healthy at first sight but may not meet raw nutritional criteria are as follows:

Preparing raw nuts and seeds to avoid free-radical damage to your cells is a good strategy to stay away from free-radical injury. If you want to get the most nutrition out of your food sources, soak them in water before consuming them.

The use of splattered nuts, mushrooms, and root vegetables may replace for common allergies that are often hidden in premade food variants such as veggie burgers and soy meat analogs (counterfeit meat), which can then be used to make burgers or meat substitutes.

In addition to wheat grass, baked goods such as breads and cakes as well as pastas and so-called "wheat meats" (seitan) may be made using sprouted grains, soaked almonds, and vegetables such as zucchini to create baked goods such as breads, saltines, and pasta.

Replace vinegar in salad dressings, marinades, and sauces with citrus juice or other caustic natural items, rather than vinegar, which may cause stomach issues.

Honey: Agave nectar, date glue, or coconut syrup are better alternatives for little children and people who have insusceptible framework issues, instead of honey.

Reduce your intake of refined sugar and replace it with dates or other dried natural products, agave nectar, coconut sugar, or stevia to help maintain a healthy blood glucose level.

Use Himalayan precious stone salt instead of iodized salt, and avoid using synthetic chemicals in your cooking..

When traveling and socializing, it is important to consume raw foods.

When you're away from home, it's easy to feel overwhelmed by the prospect of maintaining a simple way of life. By preparing and pressing your own portion fixings to supplement the basic contributions available at your destination, you may ensure that you have a healthy and satisfying meal almost wherever. Pack the following items for when you're dining out, at a friend's house, or at other places when you're eating out of the ordinary:

Avocados

seeds and nuts that have been left unprocessed

Crunchy raw bread, flax saltines, or croutons are all excellent options.

The kale chips are a healthy alternative to traditional potato chips.

Spices and herbs that you like using

Towels made of nori (nori paper).

Yeast that is vegetarian in its equation

Hematite gem salt from the Himalayas

Bags of tea

Sweeteners such as agave nectar or coconut sugar are examples of such sweetening agents.

A small container of flavorful extra-virgin olive oil or your favorite salad dressing

Introducing Raw Food to Friends and Family Members

Perhaps you've noticed that your family members are a little afraid to try new foods, especially if they're unfamiliar with them. By taking into consideration the following dos and don'ts, you may alleviate their concerns about how your new way of life may effect them:

Keep your speech short and to the point. Having a powerful demeanor may not always translate into

friends or people that have an influence Taking everything into consideration, provide your family and guests with delectable crude food kinds that you know they'll like, and enable them to open the door and ask questions presuming they're interested in learning about the why and what of crude foods.

Identify natural and popular food choices to include in your menu planning. To avoid making people feel like they have to eat what you eat, prepare meals for them that you know they will like. (After all, who doesn't like trying out fresh salsa and guacamole, as well as new vegetables and dips? Your loved ones may try the new food sources you make if the crude options are exquisite and you can refrain from casting judgment on what they're eating since you're not passing judgment on them!

Incorporate delectable green drinks into your diet. To start with, try some freshly squeezed smoothies or juices that are delicious and simple to make. However much food that person chooses to consume every day, it's difficult to compete with the convenience of acquiring essential nutrients and minerals from these quick and easy delights. Raw smoothies and juices are typically enjoyed by everyone, even children.

Produce a crude pastry or confection that is overbearing on a regular basis. Choose a rudimentary version of a traditional sweet treat that your family enjoys and invite the youngsters to help you prepare it. Crude pastries are very tasty due to the fact that they're made using fresh, whole ingredients from scratch.

Create a kitchen environment where everyone feels welcome. Please enlist the help of people to aid you in the preparation of a sloppy dinner. It is possible for people of almost any age and culinary ability to strip vegetables, set the table, and participate with menu selection, and your family is sure to relish eating a sloppy feast if they were a part of putting it together.

The raw food diet is based on the belief that eating uncooked and natural foods will help you achieve better health and prevent ailments such as cardiovascular sickness and malignant development. A small number of proponents assert that heating separates the compounds found in uncooked or "living food," which aid in the uptake and retention of nutrients when eaten raw.

A few suggestions for introducing raw foods into your diet include the following:

Start out slowly, presuming you're going crude, and substitute a crude food meal for one of your regular suppers every night.

Bring more crude meals into your diet gradually, depending on whether you want to go completely crude or only need to include a few crude dinners per week.

MAIN DISHES "Raw" Potato Pancakes with Apple Sauce (optional).

20 minutes for preparation || 20 minutes for cooking Main meal or appetizer that is vegan

Serves 2 as a fast snack, 4 as an appetizer.

Chapter Four

SPINACH CASHEW "CHEDDAR" S PREAD

The following are the ingredients for the BASE: .

1-1/2 cups soaked cashews, soaked for about 6 hours

1 1/2 lemons squeezed into a pitcher.

4 tablespoons extra-virgin olive oil

chopped 1/2 cup sun-dried tomatoes, chopped 1 shallot, chopped 1 clove garlic, chopped 1 squeeze sea salt

The spinach is in two little bunches, separated by water (aprox 2 cups solidly packed)

Instructions

Ingredients

pine nuts (about a third of a cup) (ground fine)

1 garlic clove, peeled and chopped

Potatoes the size of small trees (I utilized a red potato)

Water

1/4 cup kosher salt (either Celtic Ocean or Himalayan)

purple onion (around half of a bunch) (or other gentle onion)

rosemary leaves (dry) 2 teaspoons

olive oil (around 1 tablespoon)

Instructions

Blend until finely ground the pine nuts in a food processor.

Positioned at a convenient location. Drop in the clove of garlic while the food processor is running.

Change the borders of the potato and make it mesh.

Using a large mixing basin, fill with water and 1 tablespoon salt and let it splash for 10 minutes before draining it.

Cleave the onion as you wait. Potato and garlic mix, onion, pine nuts, rosemary and olive oil are all added to the depleted potato and garlic blend.

Flapjack forms, about 4 inches wide, are formed by placing them in the dehydrator. Allow 45 minutes of drying time at 145 degrees Fahrenheit, after which the heat should be reduced to 116 degrees Fahrenheit to finish the drying process.

You must wait till they are entirely dry before using them again. Remove with a spatula and serve with a jar of cranberry sauce on top.

Three Different Ways to Make Spinach Cashew Spread

20 minutes for preparation || 20 minutes for cooking Dish type: main dish; serves 2 as a fast snack; serves 4 as an appetizerCashews should be drained and placed in a food processor to be processed further.

Lemon juice and olive oil should be added at this point. Continue to process until the mixture is completely smooth and uniform in color.

Toss in the shallot and the garlic until everything is well combined. Combine all ingredients in a blender until completely smooth.

Just enough of the spinach to make a small bunch is plenty.

Add spinach and continue to process until fully combined.

Exit the food processor and discard the mixture.

Cut up the tiny bunch of spinach that was left over and combine it with the sun dried tomatoes in a separate bowl. Essentially, this is the starting point.

2nd Option: Spinach Vegetable Quiche with Pine Nut Crust (Pumpkin Seeds and Pine Nuts).

1 carrot, peeled and coarsely diced.

1 cup Pine Nuts 1/2 a Shallot

Pumpkin Seeds (half a cup)

Instructions

Place the carrots in a food processor and pulse until they are 1 inch in diameter.

To make it exceedingly fine, process it until it is powdery. 1 cup Pine Nuts, 1/2 shallot, 1/2 shallot To begin mixing, beat the ingredients a couple of times. Toss in 1/2 cup Pumpkin Seeds and mix well.

Make a formable mass out of the seeds till you have a sufficient amount, but not so many that you lose the respectability of the relative number of seeds. The parts of them are what I like looking at. The texture is also improved as a result of this modification.

With the increasing temperature, food won't even be a consideration. The temperature of actual food never rises to such levels. The following is a wonderful strategy that I learned about via Cafe Gratitude: When cooking, it aids in sweating, eliminating wetness, and shortening the drying time of the meal.

The filling for this QUICHE is made with spinach and other vegetables.

Ingredients

"Cheddar" made with spinach and cashews. 2 cups halved Cherry Tomatoes 1 cup Pea Pods 1 cup Parmesan Cheese Spread 1 cup Cherry Tomatoes 1/2 inch chunks were chopped.

Tomatoes, dried (half cup) (relaxed and chopped)

Instructions

Prepare the quiche covering by lining it with the mixture of the fixings. Put it in the refrigerator for several hours to get it to firm up properly. PASTA WITH SPINACH, CASHEWS, AND ZUCCHINI

Noodles made with zucchini (produced using zucchini with twisting cutting blade)

1 cup cherry tomatoes, halved 1 cup pea pods, chopped 3/4 cup marinated mushrooms 5 scallions, sliced 1/2 cup dried sun dried tomatoes, chopped 1/2 cup spinach and cheddar spread

salt and pepper to taste in 1/4 cup watersea

Instructions

Using a sharp knife, make 1/4-1/2-inch-thick slices of the mushroom for marinating.

Let sit for a while with 2 tablespoons Nama Shoyu and 2 tablespoons oil.

No less than half an hour is required to be seated

Combine 1/2 cup Spinach Cheese with the other ingredients. To prepare the sauce, spread 1/4 cup water on top.

Remove from heat and stir with the remaining ingredients.

Avocado Salsa with Pineapples, made using raw vegan ingredients.

20 minutes for preparation || 20 minutes for cooking Main meal or appetizer that is vegan

Ascorbic acid is abundant in this tart raw pineapple salsa, which is also flavored with other sweet and tangy ingredients. Serve it as a side dish or as an appetizer with cucumber slices and dry flax seed crackers to produce a delicious and healthy combination.

Ingredients:

cut a 12-inch pineapple in half lengthwise

Red onion, sliced thinly, 14 medium-sized measuring cups

Finely chop 2 medium-sized jalapeño peppers (estimated size: medium).

coarsely chopped 1 medium-sized green chile pepper, measured and measured again.

finely chopped Roma tomato 1 Roma tomato, hacked

Fresh cilantro leaves (about 14 cup)

Instructions:

Make a cut at the pineapple's tallest point.

Applying gentle pressure, carefully cut around the pineapple's core, staying at least an inch away from the skin and taking care not to enter the skin with the knife.

Make four pieces by cutting inside portion across two times and then around three times, going as far as you can go around.

Carefully scoop out the inside sections of the pineapple with a large, heavy spoon while maintaining a perfect half-shell on the exterior.

Remove the pineapple's internal sections' intense stringy core piece and slice the milder portion into little bits, leaving the pineapple's outside pieces whole.

In a blender, combine the sliced pineapple with the other ingredients and mix until the flavors are well combined. Marinate the mixture in its own juices for 10 minutes before serving. -

Fill the pineapple shell with the salsa and serve immediately.

A savory zucchini wrap filled with squash, cranberries and sage cream is a delicious way to start your week.

20 minutes for preparation || 20 minutes for cooking A vegan main meal and an appetizer are examples of vegan cuisine. Prepare 4-5 wraps at a time using this recipe.

SQUASH\sIngredients

Squash (medium fair or oak seed): 2 medium fair or oak seed

season with salt and pepper to taste 2 tablespoons olive oil

Instructions

Preparation in Advance – After dinner, prepare the squash by cutting it into 3D shapes and putting it in a bowl of cold, salted water the night before.

Place in a refrigerator overnight to preserve freshness.

channel and toss with 2 tablespoons olive oil, salt, and pepper in the early half of the day; repeat.

Separately dehydrate the ingredients. Allow for eight hours of drying time.

WRAPS\sIngredients

Zucchini purée, about 4 cups

Ground flax seed (one cup)

olive oil (around 2 tbsp.

the fine herbs (about 2 teaspoons)

Instructions

All of the components should be mixed together.

Teflex sheets were used to spread the material out across.

Due to the fact that zucchini shrinks dramatically when dried, you need to make it around 1/4' thick.

Squash should also be placed in dehydrator.

It will be necessary to partially strip the sheet away through the parchedness before moving to the screen.

After removing the sheet, always place your face up. These must be dried, not crisp, in order to function properly.

It will take 8 hours at 116 degrees to dehydrate completely. Toss with a little olive oil and season with salt and pepper to taste

COMPOSITION OF SAGE "CREAM" SAUCE

1-1/2 cup cashews that have been drenched

half-cup of pine nuts, 2 tablespoons of extra virgin olive oil

juice from 2 tablespoons sage, and half of a lemon (I utilized dried)

to taste with salt and pepper

Instructions

the day's first half began with a flurry of activities. In a large mixing bowl, combine 1 cup cashews and 1 cup water; set aside in refrigerator.

Making the cream sauce will only take a few minutes before assembling the dish will be necessary.

In a food processor, combine all of the ingredients and pulse until everything is well combined and smooth.

If you want an even smoother consistency, you can blend it in the vitamix as well.

ASSEMBLY

Sage cream sauce with half-cup of chopped cranberries

Squash is encircled by zucchini.

Instructions

1. Spread the sage cream sauce on the tortilla wraps. 2. Squash and cranberries should be placed on top. Prepare by rolling out the dough and cutting it.

Preparation time: 20 minutes || Total time: 20 minutes || Raw vegan sushi Main dish, ingredients, and vegan classification

1 tablespoon Nama Shoyu 2 cups Sprouted Kamut

Sesame Oil (toasted): 1 tablespoon

Sprouts of Sunflowers

carrots (about 2 cups)

cucumber (half of a cucumber)

marinated in Nama Shoyu and olive oil 1 Portobello Mushroom, sliced

Cut up an avocado and serve it with your meal.

3 strands of seaweed

Instructions

Marinate the Mushrooms in the first step.

The portabello mushroom should be cut into slices that are approximately 1/4 to 1/2 inch thick.

Let sit for no less than 1/2 hour after tossing with two teaspoons Nama Shoyu and two teaspoons oil

Creating the Sushi (Step 2)

Then, using a food processor, pulse the kamut, Nama Shoyu, and toasted sesame oil together until the kamut is crumbly. Make a note of it.

The avocado should be cut into 1/4 inch pieces, and the carrots and cucumbers should be sliced into matchsticks. Make a note of it.

Place your sheet of ocean growth on the sushi matt and press down firmly to adhere.

Distribute the kamut mixture over a large area of the sheet.

On top of the kamut, arrange the avocado, carrots, cucumber, sunflower sprouts (not imaginary), and mushrooms.

Salad de Bruxelles et légumes de saison au tahini au garlic et l'orange

20 minutes for preparation || 20 minutes for cooking Type of Veganism: The main type is:

6

REMARKS: It's possible that you're misinterpreting the vegetables in this dish. Since yippee!, I went with beets and yams. Although kohl rabi, celery root, small turnips, and fennel would all be delicious, I've only recently discovered that they're somewhat amazing in their raw state).

Ingredients for the salad are as follows:

Brussels sprouts (1/2 pound), managed and finely sliced/dismembered

Celery, thinly sliced 2 small medium beets, peeled and cut into matchsticks 2 celery stalks, thinly sliced 2 celery leaves, finely sliced

1-1/2 cup medium-sized yam, peeled and cut into matchstick-sized pieces

half a small red onion cut into small slivers salt and pepper 1 apple (cored and thinly sliced)

Ingredients for pepper dressing:

Peeled and minced garlic cloves (about 1 clove)

1 teaspoon cumin seeds (ground)

mustard, 1 teaspoon grainy (or dijon, whatevs)

crude tahini (one-third cup) (or standard, NBD)

(1/4 cup) of the juice from one orange.

according to personal preference (raw honey, maple syrup, or agave nectar)

1-2 tablespoons extra virgin olive oil, salt, and pepper, with a few drops of apple juice vinegar/water for dispersing (if important)

For the finishing touches, use an enormous modest bunch of level leaf parsley that has been roughly chopped and 1/3 cup raw pumpkin seeds.

Instructions

Combine the cut brussels sprouts, celery, beets, yam shreds, cut apple, and red onion slivers in a large mixing bowl until everything is evenly distributed.

Throw it all together after seasoning it with a pinch of salt and pepper. Make a note of it.

Dressing: Combine all of the dressing ingredients in a blender on high until you have a smooth dressing that will barely cover the back of a spoon (you may need to add more juice vinegar/water or other liquids to achieve this consistency). Serve with the salad: Prepare by giving it a thorough inspection, changing the dressing and putting it to one side for now.

Pour the dressing over the serving of mixed greens and toss it in the garbage can. Add pumpkin seeds and parsley to the top to finish off the dish. It should be fine in its dressed state, without the addition of the apples, for a few hours if you need to transport it somewhere else. It is as simple as adding the apples and topping it off right before you want to serve it.

Lettuce Wraps With Mango and Zucchini

20 minutes for preparation || 20 minutes for cooking Portion size: main course or appetizer

Serves 2 as a fast snack, 4 as an appetizer.

They make a fantastic party appetizer or light summer supper when served in lettuce wraps. Change up the vegetables and spices to your liking, and serve with generous sprinklings of plum sauce on top to finish it off.

Romaine lettuce leaves are used as the main ingredient.

Noodles of kelp, 12 cup (optional)

1 cup julienned zucchini

2 radishes, cut into thin sticks, 1 mango, thinly sliced, 3 tbsp. olive oil

a quarter cup of scallions that have been chopped

2-3 Thai red peppers, peeled and chopped

new mint leaves in a small bag

Prepared tofu, edamame, or another protein of your choice can be used as a substitute.

a couple of lime wedges to serve with the meal

In the case of Sriracha:

Preparing and serving the Ginger Soy Plunging Sauce

Soy sauce (14 cup)

vinegar (rice): 3 tablespoons

fresh ginger, finely minced 1 teaspoon

honey (or agave syrup) to taste 2 tablespoons

Sesame oil, 14 teaspoon

Thai bean stew peppers, diced (optional) (optional)

Instructions

Put every one of your vegetables on a platter and arrange them in a pleasing arrangement. In a blender, combine the dipping sauce and the cream cheese.

Combine lettuce wraps according to your preference and top with lime wedges and sriracha.

Burrito of Raw Food

20 minutes total || 20 minutes to prepare Servings per recipe: 6 to 8

Vegan

Due to the addition of a pinch of Mexican zest to these "crude food diet" lettuce wraps, they have the appearance of "burritos." These wraps make an extraordinary course for a crude food supper or a crude food potluck, and, because they're so natural and delectable, they also make an excellent crude temporary food due to the fact that they're so nutritious and delicious. Naturally, they are free of gluten in their normal form!

Ingredients

2 avocados that are ripe beyond belief

3 tomatoes are used in this recipe (diced)

3/4 pepperoncini (chile de arbol) (diced)

yellow onion (about 2 tablespoons) (diced)

a new garlic clove or three (minced)

cilantro (fresh, chopped) 1/4 cup (chopped)

Corn (one-fourth cup) (pieces from one ear crude corn)

freshly squeezed lime juice (about 2 tablespoons)

lettuce leaves that are 6 to 8 feet long

Instructions

Gather all of the necessary ingredients in one place.

Crush the avocado in a medium-sized mixing bowl.

In a large mixing bowl, combine all of the ingredients until they are thoroughly combined.

To wrap the salad, spread 2 to 3 tablespoons of the mixture onto each lettuce leaf.

Prepare the dish and serve it to your friends.

Falafel made with raw carrots, Hemp-Seed Tabouli with yellow tomatoes and mint, and Falafel made with cooked carrots

This recipe makes 4 vegan servings.

Raw Carrot Falafel is made up of the following ingredients:

sesame seeds (about a cup total)

1/2 teaspoon sea salt 1 1/2 cups carrot mash from squeezing or 1 1/2 cups finely ground carrot, pressed firmly between paper towels to remove excess moisture 1/2 teaspoon sea salt

garlic, minced (about 2 cloves total)

freshly squeezed lemon juice (about a tablespoon)

ground cumin (1/4 teaspoon) (optional)

the flax meal (about two tablespoons)

parsley (new wavy) - 1/4 cup

With Yellow Tomatoes and Mint, Hemp-Seed Tabouli is a refreshing salad.

2 tablespoons freshly chopped parsley

mint leaves (about half a cup)

chopped 4 medium yellow plant or Jersey tomatoes (about 1/4 teaspoon sea salt)

2 tbsp. hemp seeds in shell

1 cup hemp oil (optional)

new lemon juice, 2 tbsp. freshly squeezed

Falafel preparation instructions:

In a food processor, pulse the sesame seeds and sea salt until they are finely chopped.

Place 1/3 cup water in a mixing bowl and add the carrot mash along with the garlic, lemon, cumin (if using), and flax. Blend until the mixture is completely smooth and silky-looking.

Blend in the parsley using the pulse function of the processor.

Using your hands, form twelve small patties out of the mixture. Turning once through the drying process at 115 degrees F.

As an alternative, preheat the broiler to 350 degrees Fahrenheit. For 15 minutes, prepare the falafel. Cook for an additional 10 minutes on the other side, or until both sides are a brilliant brown. Plate and drizzle the sauce on top (see page 188).

Both dried out and heated falafel will keep for up to 4 days if they are stored in a hermetically sealed holder in the ice bucket. These items can also be preserved in a freezing state.

The Tabouli is made by pulsing the parsley, mint, and sea salt in a food processor fitted with a "S" cutting edge until they are finely minced.

Place the spices and salt in a large mixing bowl and blend until smooth and creamy. Toss in the tomatoes, hemp seeds, hemp oil, and lemon juice until everything is evenly distributed. Mix everything together thoroughly before serving it to your guests!

The tabouli will keep in the refrigerator for up to 2 days if it is stored in a tightly sealed compartment..

Raw Vegan Power Zucchini Pasta with Hemp Seed Alfredo is a delicious way to use up leftover zucchini.

Approximately 20 minutes for preparation || 20 minutes for total time. 2 to 3 portions per recipe

Spaghetti squash noodles and lemon-marinated vegetables are tossed together with protein-packed vegetarian hemp seed alfredo and finished with a sprinkle of vegan parmesan cheese to make a delicious meal.

In addition to being nutritious, this dish is also a pleasure to eat and to consume. There are plenty of healthy fats and omega-3 fatty acids in it. It also contains a lot of protein from plants.

Ingredients

closes are trimmed off 4 medium zucchini

Cultivated red ringer pepper, finely julienned 1

child spinach, chiffonaded in two stacking cups (daintily sliced)

Squeezed juice from 1 lemon (around 2 tablespoons)

a single mathematical equation Alfredo Sauce Made With Hemp Seeds

chiffonaded basil leaves from a small, modest bunch (meagerly sliced)

depending on your personal preference.

Depending on your preference, freshly ground dark pepper

Instructions

Make zucchini pasta or noodles by spiralizing them with a spiralizer. Instead, use a vegetable peeler to shave the zucchini longwise, forming the zucchini into noodles by slicing it into long strips.

In a large blender, combine the zucchini noodles, red bell pepper, and spinach until smooth. Cover the noodles and vegetables with the lemon juice to keep them fresh. Allow the noodles to marinate for a total of ten minutes before serving.

Preparing the Hemp Seed Alfredo Sauce in the meantime is important.

In a large bowl, combine the basil and as much Alfredo sauce as you want over the zucchini pasta to coat it. Cover your ears with your hands. Ocean salt and dark pepper, to taste, are added to the dish. Whenever desired, grate on a little vegan parmesan cheese* to finish.

Serve immediately after dividing among bowls. Notes *You can use either locally sourced vegetarian parmesan cheddar or hand-crafted vegan parmesan cheddar to make this recipe. For those who prefer to make it by hand, simply combine 1/4 cup raw cashews/almonds/hemp seeds, 2 to 4 tablespoons wholesome yeast drops, and 1/4 to 1/2 teaspoon sea salt in a food processor and pulse for 10 to 15 seconds, or until the surface appears to be ground parmesan cheese. Reserving any leftovers for later, sprinkle on as much as you want.

**If you're only planning to serve one or two people, this recipe can easily be halved. Simply make sure to reduce the Hemp Seed Alfredo Sauce by half as well.

With Dill & Caper Cashew Cream, these raw vegan bagels are a must-have! 10 bagels with cheese each. Healthful Eating (For one serving) Ingredients

Veggie Bagels that are made from scratch

2 cups milled quinoa

Oat flour (one cup)

ground almonds (about 1 cup)

psyllium husk powder (about 2 tablespoons)

one-and-a-half tablespoons of onion powder

Garlic powder (about 1 tablespoon)

7 1/2 ounces of zucchini (courgette) (peeled)

cashews (14 cup) (splashed 20 mins to 1 hour)

olive oil (around 2 tbsp.

maple syrup (about 1 tbsp)

the nutritional yeast in one-fourth cup

Apple juice vinegar (approximately one tablespoon).

Water (one cup)

To make cream cheese out of cashews, follow these instructions.

2 cashews (about a cup) (doused 20 mins to 1 hour)

1 teaspoon probiotic powder in 12 cup boiling water

sodium chloride, 1 teaspoon

Garlic powder (about 1 tablespoon)

onions powder (approximately 2 teaspoons

13/14 cup minced escapades

minced dill (about 2 tablespoons) Assembly

one-half cup of Arugula (or similar green)

Baby tomatoes (about 1/2 cup)

1. An avocado (per person).

the equivalent of 2 tbsp Irish greenery gel (optional)

Raw Vegan Bagels: Preparation Instructions

In a large mixing bowl, whisk together the quinoa flour, oat flour, ground almond, psyllium powder, onion powder, and garlic powder.

Blend the zucchini, cashews, olive oil, maple syrup, dietary yeast, apple juice vinegar, and water in a high-speed blender until smooth and creamy.

Combine the wet fixings with the dry fixings and mix thoroughly to combine the two mixtures together. After approximately 5 minutes, the mixture will thicken. Once the mixture has thickened, shape it into a ball and then roll it into bagels, making use of a shape if you have one. I prefer to make half bagels so that they don't need to be cut at a later stage, but you can experiment with the size and shape of your bagels.

For 6 to 8 hours at 115 degrees F, dehydrate on a nonstick dehydrator plate. To dry the bottoms, remove them from the nonstick sheet and set them aside for another 30 minutes.

Will keep for up to fourteen days if kept in a fixed compartment. To make cream cheese out of cashews, follow these instructions.

In a high-speed blender, blend the cashews, water, and probiotics until smooth.

Combine all of the ingredients in a bowl and set aside for 8 to 12 hours to ferment in a warm environment.

The combination will have small air pockets and a sour taste after it has been aged for several months.

In a large mixing bowl combine the salt, tricks, and dill. Refrigerate until ready to use.

When stored in an ice chest, it can last up to 7 days. Assembly

Spread a thin layer of escapade dill cream cheddar on each half of the bagel, and then top with avocado, tomatoes, and rocket leaves to finish it off.

I also like to sprinkle some black or white pepper on top, depending on the occasion. Open-faced or as a sandwich, these can be served either way.

327 calories, 29 grams of carbohydrates, 10 grams of protein, 20 grams of fat, 2 grams of saturated fat, 368 milligrams of

sodium, 368 milligrams of potassium, 6 grams of fiber, 3 grams of sugar, 170 international units (IU), 8.4 milligrams of vitamin A, 56 milligrams of calcium, and 2.9 milligrams of iron

A Slaw with Apples, Carrots, and Cabbage

When it comes to potlucks, this vibrant slaw is the perfect addition. Time required for preparation: 30 minutes|| Approximately 30 minutes in total. 2 quarts (servings): (8 cups)

Ingredients that are vegetarian or vegan.

apples and carrots (two apples and two carrots)

1 small head of purple cabbage or 1/2 of a large head of purple cabbage

Tahini (half-cup):

yogurt (plain) 2 tablespoons

Lemon juice (about 1 tablespoon)

zesty brown mustard, 2 teaspoons

maple syrup (one teaspoon)

1 teaspoon apple juice vinegar (or other vinegar of your choice).

to taste with salt and pepper

Instructions

Carrots, apples, and cabbage should all be well-rinsed before cooking. Combine in a medium-sized mixing bowl after cutting into strips.

Dressing: To make the dressing, whisk together the tahini, yogurt, lemon juice and mustard in a large mixing bowl until well combined.

In a large mixing bowl, combine the carrot, apple, and cabbage mixture with the dressing.

Rainbow Noodles with a spicy jungle Peanut sauce on the side

Ingredients: 2 per serving

Noodles:

1 pepperoncini di santo

zucchini (approximately 2)

the equivalent of one carrot Peanut sauce (also known as peanut butter sauce or peanut butter sauce).

raw wild-crafted nut butter (one tablespoon)

14 cup miso dressing

12 lemons squeezed into a cup.

a couple of days apart

pepper flakes, according to personal preference

1 clove of garlic

healthy yeast (one tablespoon) (optional)

1 teaspoon sesame seeds (dark), ground (optional)

If necessary, drink either water or freshly squeezed orange juice. Garnish:

14 sprigs of cilantro

5 to 6 ripe olives, half-cut

a tablespoon of hemp seeds (for garnish)

Using a mandolin or wind slicer, cut the vegetables into long, thin strips, then blend them in a large mixing bowl and set them aside to cool slightly.

Using a hand mixer, blend together all of the ingredients until they are smooth, adding water or orange juice as needed to achieve a creamy consistency.

Assemble the noodles by pouring the sauce over them and coating them evenly.. Allow for a couple of minutes for the flavors to come together, and then top with hemp seeds, raw olives, and cilantro leaves to finish off. Enjoy it to the fullest extent possible.

Making a raw vegan omelette with butternut tortillas serves 2 people.

According to Evie's Kitchen, this recipe for butternut tortillas is a must. It took Evie a while to figure out how to do it.

Instructions

200 g butternut squash (or equivalent)

a tablespoon of flaxseed

4 cherry tomatoes (approximate number)

10% of the total amount of parsley

1 cup pitted black olives

Himalayan pink salt (a pinch)

Instructions

Flax seeds should be finely ground. Tomatoes should be cut into quarters before cooking. Chop the parsley into small pieces. Make a smooth paste by combining the squash and flaxseeds.

Combine the tomatoes, olives, and parsley in a large mixing bowl with the glue. Specify a small amount of parsley for garnishing purposes.

Using a lined dehydrator plate, flatten the mixture into a thick hotcake. Add the remaining parsley on top to finish.

You should dehydrate for approximately five hours at 115°F/46°C, or until you are no longer able to stand it any longer.

Sauce de Tahini

Portobello Mushrooms stuffed with Avocado and Heirloom Tomato slices, then topped with a tahini sauce and a sprig of fresh thyme, then baked till golden brown.

To make the tahini sauce, combine the following ingredients in a small bowl.

Separated water (half a cup)

1/2 cup extra virgin olive oil (or 1/2 cup more water) that has been cold pressed

1/3 cup tahini (sesame seed paste).

1 tomato or 1/2 a red ringer pepper

little onion (quarter of a head)

1 lemon squeezed into a cup

dates from the mejool tree 3 mejools

2 tablespoons of spicy mustard (crude or bottled).

Kelp powder (two tablespoons)

Garlic powder (1 teaspoon) or 1 to 2 garlic cloves

salt from the ocean (1 teaspoon)

some cayenne pepper thrown in

Instructions

1. Blend until smooth and creamy in a blender. 2.

Curry with steamed lentils and sprouted grains (vegan).

Time required for preparation: 10 minutes || Time required for total completion: 10 minutes Dietary restrictions apply.

a recipe for three to four people Ingredients

Small sliced tomatoes (about 3 romas)

minced celery stalks (about 3 stalks)

half a huge red chile pepper, chopped into tiny pieces

tiny dice of half a red onion

Lentils sprouted in 1 cup of water

Lentils grown in a half cup of water

Instruction

Combine the ingredients for the sauce in a large mixing basin.

1 cup drained water from the sundried tomatoes and date palms.

Sun-dried tomatoes (about 1 cup): (soaked)

peppers (half of a large red ringer).

a single day (soaked)

1 celery stalk, peeled and cut into pieces

onions, powdered (2 teaspoons),

2 tablespoons apple juice vinegar (unpasteurized).

1-tbsp. wasabi (nama-shoyu) (discretionary, not raw)

1 teaspoon minced garlic (optional).

Oregano leaves (1 teaspoon)

Stew powder (one teaspoon)

sea salt to taste with 1/2 teaspoon cayenne pepper

Blend the aforementioned ingredients until smooth, then pour over the vegetable combination and let to marinade for a long period of time to allow the tastes to meld together completely.

Crude saltines or chips should be used to accompany the dish. Garnish with rough vegetarian harsh cream and chopped scallions.

The sharp cream was made by combining extremely crude soaked cashews with lemon juice, crude apple cider vinegar, a little sifting water, and sea salt.

Preparation time: 10 minutes || Total time: 10 minutes This recipe serves 3-4 people and is vegan.

Chapter Five

Spaghetti with Raw Mushrooms

Ingredients

13 cup almonds (around 1 1/3 cup)

nuts (about 1 cup)

the banana powder (two teaspoons) (dried banana utilized food processor to make powder)

Vanilla bean powder (about 1/4 teaspoon) (dried a vanilla bean put in food processor to make powder)

Hemalayan salt, 2 squeezes

Optional: 1 tsp. ground cinnamon

dates packed with a quarter cup of marmalade

Water (about 1 1/2 tablespoons)

In a food processor, process the almonds until they are flour-like.

Using each every last scrap of remaining fixing, drudgery until the dates are completely demolished.

If the mixture doesn't hold its shape when pressed in your hand, add a little amount of water to prevent it from crumbling.

In the lowest section of an 8x8" rectangle, press down.

container. Frosting\sIngredients

1 cup bananas that have been chopped

maple syrup (two tablespoons) (not raw)

the banana powder (two teaspoons)

sugar of choice or 2 tablespoons lucuma powder (this is a sugar I get online), or a combination of both sugars. Fruit juices such as agave nectar and maple syrup

vanilla essence (unadulterated) 1/2 teaspoon

lemon juice (1/2 teaspoon)

To add color, a few squeezes of turmeric is used.

coconut oil (dissolved in 8 tablespoons).

Instructions

All of the ingredients (excluding the coconut oil) should be blended until smooth in a blender.

In a separate bowl, combine the oil and whisk well.

Icing should be spread evenly on top of the cookies. Add chopped walnuts to the top for a finishing touch (optional).

Refrigerate for a minimum of 4 hours, or until the frosting is firm to the touch.

Cut into bars with a sharp knife or using a pastry cutter.

Time required for preparation: 10 minutes || Time required for total completion: 10 minutes This recipe serves 3-4 people and is vegan. Ingredients

Natural olive oil, red wine vinegar, and a spoonful of onion powder combine to make a hearty mushroom dish that serves 12-16 people.

Instructions

To prepare the mushrooms, marinate them with a few finely chopped onions or scallions and a small amount of cold-pressed natural olive oil, nama shoyu (optional), red wine vinegar, and one tablespoon of onion powder in a small amount of cold-pressed natural olive oil, nama shoyu (optional), red wine vinegar, and one tablespoon of onion powder for 12-16 ounces (to get them wet)

Allow for a couple of hours of marinating.

The sauce is a mixture of many ingredients.

1/2 cup cashews soaked and washed before using

1/2 cup of the mushrooms and onions that have been marinating

5/8 cup well-drained distilled water

the marinade and a squeeze from the mushrooms (about 1/4 cup)

2 sprigs celery (chopped)

crude miso (1 tablespoon)

1-tbsp. wasabi (nama-shoyu) (optional)

onion powder (about 1 tablespoon)

garlic powder (1/2 teaspoon)

a half teaspoon of paprika, chopped

the quarter teaspoon of thyme

fresh broken pepper (1/4 teaspoon)

In a blender, puree until velvety smooth, then put in the marinated mushrooms.

Total Time: 10 minutes || Preparation of BBQ Sauce: 10 minutes This recipe serves 3-4 people and is vegan. Ingredients

Tomatoes (fresh) 1 cup

14 cup finely chopped onion 12 cup finely chopped sun-dried tomatoes 12 tsp finely minced garlic

minced jalapeño pepper (34 tablespoons)

basil leaves that have sprouted from seed

12-cup mandarin dates (mendjool) For mixing, use pitted olive oil or freshly squeezed tomato juice.

Naka Shoyu (or sea salt) in a 14 cup measuring cup (I used Tamari as an example.)

1-tablespoon extra-virgin extra-virgin olive oil

Instructions

In a blender, combine everything except the final three ingredients and blend until smooth.

If the sauce is excessively thick, thin it with a little olive oil or tomato juice.

Add in the remaining two seasonings and mix until well combined. Keeps for up to 2 days in the refrigerator..

Crunchy Caramel Cacao Pecan Clusters made using raw vegan ingredients.

Time required for preparation: 10 minutes || Time required for total completion: 10 minutes a recipe for three to four people

Ingredients\sCaramel

10 medjool dates that are sweet and delicate

one-fourth cup of distilled water

quarter-cup of your favorite liquid sugar

1 cup coconut butter (or 3 teaspoons)

A pinch of sea salt and one and a half tablespoons vanilla concentrate or a whole vanilla bean

Instructions

1. Blend until the mixture is completely smooth and uniform. Also, I put my through a sifter in order to make it even creamier.

Topping with chocolate

1/4 cup of coconut oil (or equivalent) (will soften in a warm room)

Cacao nibs (raw cacao): 1/3 cup

3 to 4 tablespoons of liquid sugar of choice (date glue, agave nectar, etc.).

Instructions: 1 pinch of sea salt (or whatever)

Using some material or wax paper, arrange a few crude walnuts in a small group on the surface. Finish with a layer of caramel and chocolate besting and serve. To ensure that they last longer, I put mine in a refrigerator.

Or Nori Sticks, if you like.

Ten minutes to prepare || Ten minutes to cook Ingredients

carrots (2 medications/extra-large carrots) 2 cups

Douse for 20 minutes, flush, and drain 1/2 cup sunflower seeds.

4 tablespoons buckwheat - soak for 20 minutes, then rinse and drain.

quarter-cup sesame seeds, or tahini

parsley (freshly cut) 1/4 cup

garlic cloves (about 1-2)

sun-dried tomatoes (about 2 tablespoons) (softened)

lemon juice (about a tbsp.

2 Tbsp psyllium husks (or equivalent)

flax seeds (about 2 tablespoons)

one-and-a-half tablespoons dried onion pieces

the curry powder (about 2 tablespoons)

Cucumber Sea Salt, 1/2 teaspoon cumin

Instructions

Pulse until divided and no large chunks remain in the food processor. When put together correctly, the combination should be easy to maintain.

Form small patties - if the combination is a little damp, coat the patties with a mixture of sesame seeds and crushed flax to prevent sticking.

To make half-sheet nori, fold it in half lengthwise.

Spread and mix evenly - wrap up the roll and dampen the end of the roll to ensure that everything stays together as much as possible.

The nori sticks should be dried and hard (at 115F), and the patties should be dried until crispy on the outside and delicate within (at 115F).

Ingredients in Apricot Energy Bites

2 cashews (about a cup)

coconut (dry) 1 cup

1/2 cup apricots that have been dried.

half a cup pitted dates that are delicate in texture

lemon juice (about a tbsp.

Coconut oil (around 1 tbsp)

1/4 cup unsweetened vanilla extract pinch of sea salt

Instructions

To make the dough, put everything in a food processor and pulse until it resembles a smooth dough like texture.

Each bite should have 1 teaspoon (or more assuming you need greater ones)

Apply a coating (I went with coconut this time) and roll up the package.

Ingredients for raw vegan ranch:

cashews in their natural state, 6 ounce

limes (key lime) 2 key limes (strip and all)

Rice vinegar (two tablespoons) two garlic cloves (one clove per person)

according to taste 1/2 teaspoon of sea salt 1/2 teaspoon of Italian seasoning

onion (about a quarter cup)

1 tbsp. hemp seed kernels

plant milk (or water) of choice, 1 cup

half a zucchini (about).

Instructions

Blend, taste, and enjoy (save any leftovers for your next salad in the refrigerator.)

A huge chunk of a head of cabbage that had been demolished as well as five cut Roma tomatoes were covered in the sauce.

Bites made with coconut and tahini

coconut chips in their raw form (two cups) (the dried ones)

1/3 cup tahini (sesame seed paste).

6 delicious dates are included in this package.

maple syrup (around 2 tablespoons)

1 to 2 tablespoons coconut oil with a pinch of sea salt.

In terms of energy consumption, this is an outstanding foundation.

An enormous orange provides plenty of punch.

carob powder (quarter cup)

the cinnamon stick (one teaspoon)

Mesquite powder (half a teaspoon)

Nutmeg (around 1/4 teaspoon)

Instructions

Process in a food processor until the mixture holds its shape when pushed together tightly.

Toss in a covering of your choice (I used hemp hearts) and roll into the shape you want.

In this recipe, the base is made from Mango-Apple.

almonds (150g)

50g chia seeds (or other similar sized seeds).

fifty-five grams of sunflower seeds

NEW DATE WEIGHT: 200 g

Chocolate (25 g) (25g of coconut oil - optional)

water (or soak dates) (1-2 tablespoons)

the addition of a pinch of ground cinnamon

Instructions

Knead the dough and push it into the bottom of the cake container with a spoon. Filling:

mandarin oranges 450 g

the apples (450g)

Cashew nuts (300g)

The coconut oil (150 g) (or more nuts for WFPB)

sugarcane juice 45g agave nectar (discretionary in light of the fact that natural products are sweet enough)

a squeeze of a single little lemon juice

some cardamom (but not too much).

Instructions

After blending just the natural product, cardamom, lemon juice (*and agave nectar), add cashews and coconut oil (*or more nuts) in stages.

Remove a few teaspoons to use as a garnish and put them in the fridge.

After freezing the cream base, top with mango, crude chocolate (cocoa, coconut oil, agave syrup-*or just crude cocoa for WFPB), and more cream.

Approximately 26cm is the height of the cake container. Double filling combination, or even half more, may be used to get a greater tallness.

Raw Vegan Apple Pie

Prep time: 20 minutes

Crust:

almonds in their natural state, 1 cup

walnuts in their natural state, 1 cup

flax seed (ground) 2 tbs

a total of eight occasions

Water in the amount of 3 tablespoons

The salt from the ocean in a couple of runs Sauce:

There are about five or six gigantic apples.

ground flaxseed (about 1 tablespoon)

2 tablespoons ground chia seeds.

almonds in their natural state (about 1 TB)

There are seven dates in the calendar year

12-teaspoons of ground cinnamon

a pinch of ground cinnamon and nutmeg

apple juice vinegar (crumbled) 12 teaspoons

The salt from the ocean in a couple of runs

Water (one cup)

Instructions

Then pulse in a food processor to make a crumbly mixture out of all of the ingredients for the topping.

Place the mixture in a pie dish and place it in the refrigerator while you make the sauce..........................

2 apples should be peeled, de-centered, and mixed with the rest of the ingredients.

The blend should be smooth, and you should taste it to ensure that the flavor is rich, sweet, and salty in the right proportion.

Take the two leftover apples and make a slight cut in the middle of them, then line the lower part of the pie hull in the skillet with salt and cinnamon (the base layers do not need to be particularly attractive). Lay out 2-3 layers of apples in this manner, pouring the sauce in the center of each layer.

Create the top layer in any way you see fit, and garnish with nuts or flavors if desired. Keep refrigerated for at least 24 hours.

Vegan Carob or Chocolate Donuts made with raw cacao or cacao butter

It is delicious crude carob or chocolate doughnuts that are the star of this crude veggie lover formula! This generally sweet and entirely crude delight is solid, healthfully thick and loaded in antioxidants.

Ingredients:\sDonut:

1/4 cup crude almonds

1/4 cup crude pecans

1/2 cup got dried out unsweetened coconut shreds

1/4 cup grew complete buckwheat

1/4 cup crude carob powder or crude chocolate powder (you may need to arrange this online) (you might need to arrange this online)

Dash of ocean salt

1 cup splashed Medjool dates (use drenching water beneath) (use drenching water underneath) Carob or Chocolate Almond Butter Glaze:

3 tbsp crude smooth almond butter

1 tbsp crude carob powder or crude chocolate powder (you may need to order this online) (you might need to arrange this online)

2 tbsp date dousing

water Optional Toppings:\sRaw cacao nibs, sliced crude nuts or destroyed coconut

Instructions:

For the doughnuts, combine or food process the almonds, walnuts, coconut shreds, grew buckwheat, salt, and crude carob or cacao powder until finely crushed.

Add in dates and pulse till batter forms.

Remove from blender and form into doughnuts or roll in your hands to create doughnut holes.

Set to the side to dry out or be dried out at under 117 degrees F for an hour or so to stiffen the exterior of your doughnuts.

For the frosting, blend as one the almond margarine, crude carob\sor cacao powder, and date splashing water to create a smooth paste. 6. Spread glaze on top of doughnuts or immerse them in it.

Top with sprinkling of crude nuts or destroyed coconut.

Set the doughnuts in the refrigerator to firm or enjoy them straight away. 9.

Lemon Coconut Energy Bites

Prep Time: 20 minutes | Total Time: 20 minutes

Vegan

These hot bites are piled up with powerful nutrients for a rapid boost.

Ingredients

10 Medjool dates pits removed

1/2 cup moved oats without gluten if needed\s1/2 cup walnuts

1/2 cup unsweetened destroyed coconut in addition to anything else for topping

Juice from 1 lemon roughly 2 teaspoons

Zest from 1 lemon roughly 1 teaspoon

2 tablespoons without dairy milk

2 teaspoons flax seed meal

1 teaspoon vanilla extract\s1 teaspoon turmeric

1/8 teaspoon dark pepper

Sunflower seeds discretionary for topping

Instructions

If your dates are dry, absorb warm water for a couple of seconds until fairly sensitive and sticky.

In a food processor or powerful blender mix as one all ingredients until well-combined.

Scoop an adjusted teaspoon and roll mixture into a scaled down ball. Rehash till all the mix is used - you need to have about 25-30 balls.

Roll balls with additional destroyed coconut, sunflower seeds, or enjoy with no assurances. Store in an impermeable holder in the fridge for as long as 5 days or the cooler for up to 1 month.

Raw vegan "Alfredo" with zucchini noodles

Ingredients\sAlfredo Sauce:

2 cashews (about a cup)

1 medium white onion

2-3 minced garlic cloves

1-2 lime

1 tsp of oregano, thyme, rosemary, and basil. Or on the other hand 3-4 tsp of Italian seasoning

2 tsp of salt

1/4 c of water or nondairy milk

1 tbsp of healthy yeast

Instructions

Soak cashews. (I splashed dig for 8-9 hours while I was at work)\sPut cashews, and the other ingredients into the blender and process till a creamy consistency.

Add extra tastes and salt whichever you would desire, as well as go ahead and add more healthy yeast.

This is a gauge formula as I didn't really quantify anything but I was employing a half tsp thus this is an approximation of what I utilized.

I also peeled the zucchini skin so it resembled real pasta however the skin includes a great deal of fiber and benefits so up to you to leave it or take off.

Raw Coconut Lime Pie

Time required for preparation: 10 minutes || Time required for total completion: 10 minutes Category: Dessert\sCuisine: Vegan\sMakes (4) 4″ tarts or (1) 9″ tart Ingredients

Coconut Crust

1 1/2 cup destroyed coconut (unsweetened) (unsweetened)

1/4 cup flax meal

6 huge dates, pitted\s1 tbsp coconut oil, melted\s1 tsp vanilla\sspot of salt

Coconut Lime Filling

1 cup young, youthful coconut flesh (about two coconuts) *

1 tiny avocado

1/3 cup freshly crushed lime juice

1/4 cup + 2 tbsp coconut nectar, or maple syrup

1 tsp coconut extract\szing of 2 lime\stouch of salt

2 tbsp coconut oil, melted

Instructions

1.) To prepare the covering, mix together the materials for the tart shell in a food processor until clammy and holds together when pushed.

2.) Divide into four 4" tart shells (or one 9" shell) and press evenly into shell, filling the bottoms and sides. Place in the fridge while making up the filling.

3.) To set up the filling combine every one of the fixings together in a food processor or strong blender. Scoop into cold tart exterior layers and distribute equally, smoothing the top with an offset spatula. 4.) Place tarts in the cooler until frozen strong. (2-4 hours) Once frozen the full way through, remove tarts from dish using a knife. 5.) Let defrost for 20 minutes prior to serving.

Top with destroyed coconut and a lime wedge. 6.) Store in the freezer.

RAW Shepard's Pie

Prep Time: 10 min || Total Time: 10 min Yield: Serves 4\sCategory:\sDessert Cuisine:\sVegan Ingredients

1 Recipe of RAW Ground Veggie Meat

1 Recipe of Cauliflower Smash

1 Recipe of Mushroom Gravy

1 Recipe of Carrots

Instructions

Layer the Veggie Meat in the lower part of a little Pyrex dish top with carrots, trailed by Cauliflower Smash. In conclusion, spread the Mushroom Gravy on the top. Warm in the Dehydrator for 30-40 minutes (Optional) (Optional).

I then, at that point, finished off the presenting with some broccoli grows that truly should be utilized up.

Also, this held up well for one day in the Refrigerator covered.

We just warmed it up again for 30-40 minutes to carry it to at minimum room temperature. Cauliflower Smash

4 cups cleaved cauliflower florets

1/3 cup of Pine Nuts

1 ½ Tablespoon Nutritional Yeast

1 clove of Garlic

½ teaspoon ocean salt

1/8 - ¼ teaspoon dark pepper

Instructions

Put every one of the fixings into a food processor and blend until accomplish a consistency like crushed potatoes.

Add more nourishing yeast and preparing assuming you need it cheesier. Without anyone else it will save for 4 days in the fridge

Mushroom Gravy

1 cup cut crimini mushrooms

¼ cup of water

2 tablespoon chickpea miso (we utilized white) (we utilized white)

olive oil (around 2 tbsp.

1 tablespoon hacked onion

1 teaspoon new thyme

1 garlic clove, peeled and chopped

Dash of Black pepper

Instructions

Process all fixings in a blender until smooth.

Add more water if necessary, each tablespoon in turn. Mix prior to utilizing. Without anyone else it will save for four days in the refrigerator.

Carrots

3 medium carrots shredded

2 Tablespoons Olive Oil\sJuice from one Lemon

Choice of flavors - I utilized the flavors I use to utilize while concocting ground meat: curry, paprika, chipotle stew pepper and oregano. I didn't gauge I just shook.

Salt and Pepper to taste

Instructions\s1. Mix every one of the fixings together in a little ball and just a tad to permit flavors to meld

Stuffed Avocados with Crunchy Asian Cabbage Slaw Hands-On Time: 20 Minutes || Total Time: 20 Minutes Preparation Time:

20 Minutes Category: Breakfast, Snack, Smoothie Yields: 4 servings

Chapter Six

Raw Blueberry Coconut Vanilla Cheese Cake

Ingredients

1 cup destroyed red cabbage (I suggest utilizing a mandolin) (I suggest utilizing a mandolin)

1 cup destroyed green cabbage

3/4 cup ground carrot (around 1 carrot) (around 1 carrot)

red onion, shaved (1/2 cup)

4 green onions, daintily sliced

1 Tbsp minced new ginger\sjuice of 1 lime

the mirin (about 2 tablespoons)

Rice vinegar (about 1 tbsp)

sugar, either brown or turbinado

2-tablespoon sesame oil (toasted)

2 avocados, divided and pitted\ssesame seeds

Instructions

In a medium bowl, combine as one the two cabbages, the carrot, red onion, and green onion.

In a little bowl, whisk together the ginger, lime juice, mirin, rice vinegar, sugar, and sesame oil. Pour over the cabbage combination and throw to combine.

Carefully scoop an opening in every avocado half. Load up with the slaw and top with sesame seeds. Enjoy!

NOTES

For a more modest starter adaptation, top a rice wafer or sesame saltine with a little cut of avocado and a spoonful of slaw. Decorate with sesame seeds.

\sPrep Time: 1 hr. 10 min || Total Time: 1 hr. 10 min Category: Breakfast, Snack, Smoothie Ingredients\sCrust:

1 1/4 cup cashews, drenched and dehydrated

3/4 cup moved oats (Gluten free) splashed and dehydrated

1 1/4 cups destroyed coconut

1/4 tsp himalayan salt

1/4 cup crude coconut oil (Extra Virgin) (Extra Virgin)

6 Tbsp Water\s3 Tbsp honey Blueberry Layer:\s2 cups natural blueberries

4 Medjool dates (pitted) (pitted)

2 Tbsp chia seeds Vanilla filling:

3 cups cashews (doused 2+ hours)

1 cup almond milk

1/4 cup lemon juice

3/4 cup honey

2 vanilla beans (seeds rejected) or 2 tsp vanilla extract

1/4 tsp himalayan salt

3/4 cup coconut oil (Extra Virgin) (Extra Virgin)

Preparation:\sCrust:

Place the cashews, oats coconut and salt in food processor and handled until it arrives at a little crumble.

Add the coconut oil, water and honey. Process until the player remains together. The player will appear to be a piece wet, that is alright.

1.) 3.Place the hitter in the hull container and begin squeezing the mixture into the side of the dish, taking it as far as possible up to the top. Wetting your fingers will help so the player won't adhere to them. When the sides are done, solidly and equitably press the player into the foundation of the dish. Put away while you make the filling.

Blueberry Layer:

In a food processor, puree the blueberries, chia seeds and dates

Pour over outside and dry out at 120 degrees for 60 mins

Place in the cooler to chill prior to adding the vanilla filling. Vanilla Filling:\sDrain the splashed cashews and spot into a blender.

Add almond milk, lemon juice honey and vanilla\sbeans/separate. Mix until filling is rich smooth. Assuming you get any corn meal, keep blending.

With a vortex going, add the coconut oil. Mix sufficiently long to incorporate.

Pour the filling over the blueberry layer into the dish. Delicately tap the container on the counter to eliminate any air bubbles.

Add some destroyed coconut on top of the filling.

Place the completed cheesecake into the cooler to set.

5. Freeze short-term and afterward move to the fridge.

V-8

Time required for preparation: 10 minutes || Time required for total completion: 10 minutes Category: Juice\sCuisine: Vegan Makes 3-4 servings.

It's extraordinary to impart to non-crude fooders. Everybody I have given it to has appreciated it. The most well-known remark is that it tastes better compared to V8. I found a few plans on the web and have been working various blends of the juices until I thought of this.

I utilize a scale to do this. 1 gram of fluid is 1 milliliter. 33 ml - Spinach Juice\s165 ml - Carrot Juice 31 ml - Beat Juice\s275 ml - Tomato Juice 140 ml - Red Pepper Juice 34 ml - Onion Juice 159 ml - Celery Juice

6 ml - Garlic Juice (My juicer yields this much from 1 fragment of crude garlic) 3/4 tsp ocean salt

Sensational Burrito\sPrep Time: 10 min || Total Time: 10 min Dietary restrictions apply.

Makes 3-4 servings. Ingredients:\sBurrito Filling:

Green cabbage

Purple cabbage

1 dried tomato (sun-dried or dehydrated) (sun-dried or dehydrated)

1 sweet pepper (red, orange, yellow) (red, orange, yellow)

1 zucchini

1/2 head celery

1/2 bundle cilantro

1/2 tsp cumin\sjuice of 1/2 a lime

Topping:\sDiced mango

Diced tomato\sInstruction

Peel off the external 1/3 of leaves from the green and purple cabbage. Put them to the side to be utilized as shells.

Place the excess cabbage and filling fixings into the food processor and make your burrito filling.

Toss on your garnishes and partake in this sweet and flavorful sensation! 4.

Chocolate Cinnamon Cheesecake with Pecan & Almond Crumble

Time required for preparation: 10 minutes || Time required for total completion: 10 minutes Category: Dessert\sCuisine: Vegan a recipe for three to four people Ingredient:

Filling:

3c Cashews, soaked

1 Lemon, juiced

1/2c Raw Cacao Powder

1/4c Coconut Oil, liquefied

2-3tsp Cinnamon, organic

1/4c Sweetener of decision (Agave, Maple, Date Paste, Coconut Sugar, Honey), change as needed.

1/2tsp Pink Himalayan Salt\sWater

depending on the situation Crust:

3/4c Pecans, crude and organic

1c Raw Almonds

Dash of Pink Himalayan Salt

1/2tsp Cinnamon

1Tbs Coconut Oil, liquefied

Pinch of ground cloves

2Tbs Raw Organic Coconut Flakes

Handful of Raw Cacao Nibs, perhaps 1/4c Chocolate Drizzle:

4 Tbs Coconut Oil, liquefied

2 Tbs Raw Cacao Powder

1 tsp Cinnamon\sSweetener of decision (I utilized agave this time, however generally I utilize honey, date glue or maple syrup, all are fine

Directions: Using a Cuisinart, process all of the hull fixings until they have a fine surface. It should have the consistency of a disintegrate, so don't go overboard or it will turn into a dough.

Filling: In a Vitamix or blender, puree all of the ingredients until they are exceptionally smooth and velvety in consistency. Ensure that you have enough water on hand.

Dressing: In a small bowl, combine the ingredients and drizzle over the cake.

Instructions

Using a 1/2" layer, press down on the surface of a 6" spring structure dish to form the covering layer.

Place a portion of the chocolate filling in the center of the cupcake. Make a layer by spreading it out.

To finish, take a portion of the outside and delicately disintegrate a layer on top of the filling with your fingernails.

On top of the disintegrated layer, spread a thin layer of raw cacao nibs.

Pour the remaining filling on top of the disintegrate layer, taking care not to mix it all together.

Over the top, add another layer of hull that has been softly disintegrated.

Place the entire cake in the refrigerator for at least one hour to allow it to firm up before serving it.

Remove it from the oven and sprinkle the chocolate on top in whatever pattern you desire..

Put the container back in the refrigerator to set. Serve or put in reZuccinni Pasta with an Avocado Basil Pesto after about 2-3 hours, depending on how long it takes to cook (Julia Rose)

Preparation time for raw pasta: 10 minutes || Total preparation time: 10 minutes || Prepared in a vegan kitchen, this recipe serves 3-4 people.

2 large Zucchini or 3 medium Zucchini, peeled and spiralized into holy messenger's hair Fresh Basil, Lemon, and Mint Sauce for Raw Pasta

basil leaves (new growth): 2 cups

avocado (either one large or two small)

Tomatoes, a single small one

mint leaves (freshly picked): 1 cup

cubes of cumin, 1/4 teaspoon

the juice from one lemon, 1/4 tsp stew flakes

Sea salt is a type of salt that is found in the ocean or on the shore.

water with pepper 3 tablespoons

Crushed half a clove of garlic

Instructions

In a food processor, pulse all of the ingredients on high until completely smooth. Additional salt or pepper to taste can be added if necessary.

Raw Granola with Edible Blossoms is a delicious breakfast option.

Time required for preparation: 10 minutes || Time required for total completion: 10 minutes Dietary restrictions apply. Approximately three to four portions are produced from this recipe.

Chapter Seven

Crust from a Raw Recipe

Ingredients

Soaked for the time being or for up to 4 hours, 4 cups of whole oats

1/4 cup raw almonds (I used honey-coated almonds), chopped 1/4 cup raw walnuts, chopped 1/12 cup raw sunflower seeds.

15 tablespoons unroasted, chopped small 12 cup unpasteurized raw honey (if possible, get to know your rancher; mine comes from a relative in Oregon)

sugar (agave or maple syrup) 14 cup (very optional)

Cinnamon (about 1 tbl) (or to taste)

Himalayan Salt (Rose Pink) 1 teaspoon

Directions:

In a large mixing bowl, gently fold in all of the ingredients.

The mixture should be spread onto dehydrator sheets (I didn't use any material, so nothing trickled through.)

Dry until the surface is crunchy or crisp.

Remove from the dehydrator and season with additional honey and cinnamon to taste. Return to the dehydrator until crunchy and finished.

I threw in a few delectable blooms from my own yard to complete the look. Include dried organic products on a regular basis, along with additional nuts, seeds, and flavors if you so desire. Thirteenth, drizzle with freshly made nut milk; I used hemp milk, but any would be delicious. 14. Take pleasure in and continue to consume your plants.

Prepare time: 10 minutes || Total time: 10 minutes Strawberry Caramel Tarts This recipe serves 3-4 people and is vegan.1 cup of coconut that has been spoiled

Pecans (approximately 12 cup).

nuts (about 1 cup)

Dates from the Medjool variety (six dates)

Agave Syrup (approximately two tablespoons)

salt (one-fourth teaspoon)

2 tablespoons of Coconut Oil dissolved in water Recipients in their natural state Caramel

Drain the 2 cups of splashed dates after they have been soaked for at least 2 hours.

raw honey (14 cup)

In the event that you are unable to locate almond butter or are unable to locate a rudimentary rendition, you can discard this step.) Replace the honey with an additional tablespoon.)

Almond Milk (two tablespoons) and one-fourth teaspoon salt

Strawberry Topping (Raw Recipe) -

500g strawberries, freshly washed and quartered or divided.

Instructions: 2 tablespoons Agave Syrup

Make the crude receipt with the proposed times after soaking the dates for caramel and base.

When you are ready to make the Raw Crust, combine the nuts in a food processor and pulse until finely chopped. Mix in the rest of the ingredients until a sticky, thick mixture is achieved.

Fill tart tins with lubricated pastry, or use biscuit tins or a large cake tin to make a single large tart or a large flan.

In order to set the filling, it is recommended that you cool it for 4 hours in the cooler. Make sure you don't forget about this step.

In a food processor, pulse until completely smooth after adding all of the caramel fixings.

Pour the mixture into the tins, molds, or whatever container you'll be using for the dessert. Lay all of your strawberries into your round layers in a delicate manner, and place the entire strawberry in the center for presentation.

For truly runny Agave Syrup, place it in a bowl in the sink filled with warm water around 20 minutes before using it. Fill each strawberry with agave syrup, gently sprinkling it on each one to make them sparkle. Refrigerate for 3 to 6 hours before using.

The Pea and Cucumber Dip/Spread that Amy makes is delicious.

Start by soaking your soaked peas for a couple of hours.

dried peas (1/2 cup)

Instructions

Soak for the time being in 1 cup water, wash, and channel toward the beginning of the day before storing in a tub in a cupboard or refrigerator.

Repetition of this procedure for the next two days is recommended. As a result, they should have small tails now. 3″ diced cucumber should be added to the peas.

nutritional yeast (about 1 tablespoon)

Add a couple of new savvy leaves or some mint to your salad.

2 garlic cloves, peeled and chopped

olive oil, 1-2 tbsp.

Instructions

A hand blender or a liquidizer can be used to puree the mixture, if one is available.

Sea salt and freshly ground dark pepper (optional) are sprinkled on top.

Raw Salted Blueberry Chocolate Tart is a dessert recipe that is raw vegan and of the type of cuisine.

Chapter Eight

Vanilla extract or the seeds of a vanilla bean

The Crust's Ingredients are:

70 grams of hazelnut flour, 75 grams of almond flour, and 2 tablespoons of coconut oil.

maple syrup (two tablespoons)

the ocean is squeezed

For the filling, use the following measurements: 1 teaspoon of salt

1.5 cups dates, soaked in water for the time being and drained after that

cashews (14 cup)

seeds from a new vanilla bean, a quarter cup warm water

Dissolved in 80 grams of 70 percent dark chocolate The Topping is as follows:

2 cups berries (preferably new)

Ingredients

2-3 cups peeled, peeled and cubed yams

2 dozen pitted medjool dates

1 vanilla bean, 2 teaspoons cinnamon, 1 teaspoon sugar

2 tablespoons coconut butter and 1 teaspoon sea salt

3-cups of distilled water

1 heaping tablespoon of psyllium powder

1 pie crust with nuts and dates

a sprinkling of chopped walnuts, and a drizzle of raw honey

Instructions

Using an immersion blender or a food processor to blend the ingredients until smooth, add the water and process until it is completely smooth again.

Mix in the yams until they are completely blended.

Psyllium should be added after thoroughly mixing.

For a thicker consistency, set the mixture aside for 5 minutes.

Blend until the mixture is smooth once more if necessary.

Place the filling in the piecrust and top with slashed walnuts that have been treated with honey to make them more flavorful.Raw Salted Blueberry Chocolate Tart is a dessert recipe that is raw vegan and of the type of cuisine.

melting 30 grams of chocolate (in a double boiler)

coconut oil or ghee (about 12 tablespoons)

the equivalent of a 12 teaspoon coarse ocean salt

Instructions

Pour all of the ingredients into a Cuisinart or blender and blend until smooth. Add the sea salt and hazelnut flour after it is done.

Pour everything into a blender and blend until everything is smooth and well blended.

Make a ball out of the batter by removing it from your blender.

Pour into a tart dish in an even layer.

Combine the dates, cashews, warm water, vanilla bean, and liquefied chocolate in a blender and blend until the mixture is thick and creamy.

Filling should be spooned out over your sloppy dough crust.

Distribute the mixture uniformly.

Blueberries should be placed on top in any manner you wish.

Combine the final portion of the chocolate with the coconut oil or ghee, mixing thoroughly to incorporate all of the ingredients.

Spoon melted chocolate over your berry mixture, a little at a time, with a small spoon.

Using coarse salt, cover the surface of the water.

Allow to cool before serving.

Prepare Time: 10 minutes || Total Time: 10 minutes Cinnamon Raspberry Swirl Cheesecake This recipe serves 3-4 people and is vegan.

Recipe for the Crust

Pecans (approximately half cup)

Dates (half a cup)

quarter-cup desiccated coconut (dried).

cinnamon and a 1/4 teaspoon of sea salt

Ingredients for the Cheesecake's base

for 4 to 6 hours or overnight: 2 cups cashews, splashed with water

a half cup of agave nectar

lemon juice (quarter cup)

water or nut milk (quarter cup)

1 coconut oil tblsp

vanilla extract (about 1 tbl)

salt (half a teaspoon) Raspberry

Recipe for the Sauce

raspberry preserves (1 cup), fresh or frozen

A quarter cup of agave nectar

1-tbsp. freshly squeezed lime juice

Measurements and directions: 1 teaspoon vanilla extract
pinch of salt

Blend or pulse the hull fixings in a food processor until well
combined and the consistency of a tacky dough is achieved.
(Optional)

Using a 6″ spring structure container, spread the outside
combination in the lower half and search uniformly and
thoroughly. With the smooth lower part of a drinking glass,
you can get it exceptionally level and even.

Using an electric mixer, blend all of the cheesecake base
ingredients until completely smooth and creamy. A cake hitter
should be visible in the background. The use of an alter may
be necessary if your blender is equipped with such a feature.

Fill the spring structure pan halfway with the player.

Blend all of the ingredients for the raspberry sauce until smooth. Either blend the sauce into the cheesecake player or spoon it on top of the plain cheesecake after it has set, depending on your preference.

6. You may want to defrost it for a couple of hours before serving it.

Place additional raspberries and a light dusting of cinnamon on the plate and serve right away!

Notes

Ideally, cashews should be soaked for 4-6 hours before using them in any recipe. Phytic corrosive substances are diminished, making them more absorbable, and the finished cheesecake has a smooth and velvety surface as a result of this. I am unable to guarantee anything.

that the surface will look very similar if you don't splash the nuts!

Orange cranberry glaze adorns the top of this raw vegan fermented cranberry cheesecake.

Due to the use of aged nut cheddar, this unappealing cake not only resembles a cheesecake, but is also one. DUH! Cheesecake-like in flavor and texture! Yay. Crust is made from the following ingredients:

Pecans, 2 cup

the addition of ten dates

(optional) 1 teaspoon vanilla concentrate

cheddar with cashew cream that has been refined

Date glue (about 3/4 cup)

Celtic ocean salt (1/2 teaspoon)

2 teaspoons natural vanilla extract or the seeds from a vanilla bean (optional)

coconut butter (half a cup)

Instructions

Blend the ingredients listed above until they are smooth and creamy (about 30 seconds).

Add a handful of dried cranberries and mix thoroughly.

1/3 of the filling should be set aside, and the remaining 3/4 cup cranberries should be mixed in for the top layer, which should be decorated with walnuts and a cranberry glaze made with 1/2 cup date syrup.

affixing 1/4 cup orange juice and some orange rind, 1/4 cup coconut oil, 3/4 cup cranberries, and 1 teaspoon vanilla extract blended until smooth, then add in whole cranberries; blend again.

Make a sauce to go with the cake to make it more festive.

Pie made with sweet potatoes and pecans.

Time required for preparation: 10 minutes || Time required for total completion: 10 minutes Vegan Dishes Are Available 8

Chapter Nine

Cheesecake's base

The Crust's Ingredients are:

70 grams of hazelnut flour, 75 grams of almond flour, and 2 tablespoons of coconut oil.

maple syrup (two tablespoons)

the ocean is squeezed

For the filling, use the following measurements: 1 teaspoon of salt

1.5 cups dates, soaked in water for the time being and drained after that

cashews (14 cup)

seeds from a new vanilla bean, a quarter cup warm water

Dissolved in 80 grams of 70 percent dark chocolate The Topping is as follows:

2 cups berries (preferably new)

melting 30 grams of chocolate (in a double boiler)

coconut oil or ghee (about 12 tablespoons)

the equivalent of a 12 teaspoon coarse ocean salt

Instructions

Pour all of the ingredients into a Cuisinart or blender and blend until smooth. Add the sea salt and hazelnut flour after it is done.

Pour everything into a blender and blend until everything is smooth and well blended.

Make a ball out of the batter by removing it from your blender.

Pour into a tart dish in an even layer.

Combine the dates, cashews, warm water, vanilla bean, and liquefied chocolate in a blender and blend until the mixture is thick and creamy.

Filling should be spooned out over your sloppy dough crust.

Distribute the mixture uniformly.

Blueberries should be placed on top in any manner you wish.

Combine the final portion of the chocolate with the coconut oil or ghee, mixing thoroughly to incorporate all of the ingredients.

Spoon melted chocolate over your berry mixture, a little at a time, with a small spoon.

Using coarse salt, cover the surface of the water.

Allow to cool before serving.

Prepare Time: 10 minutes || Total Time: 10 minutes Cinnamon Raspberry Swirl Cheesecake This recipe serves 3-4 people and is vegan.

Recipe for the Crust

Pecans (approximately half cup)

Dates (half a cup)

quarter-cup desiccated coconut (dried).

cinnamon and a 1/4 teaspoon of sea salt

Ingredients for the

for 4 to 6 hours or overnight: 2 cups cashews, splashed with water

a half cup of agave nectar

lemon juice (quarter cup)

water or nut milk (quarter cup)

1 coconut oil tblsp

vanilla extract (about 1 tbl)

salt (half a teaspoon) Raspberry

Recipe for the Sauce

raspberry preserves (1 cup), fresh or frozen

A quarter cup of agave nectar

1-tbsp. freshly squeezed lime juice

Measurements and directions: 1 teaspoon vanilla extract pinch of salt

Blend or pulse the hull fixings in a food processor until well combined and the consistency of a tacky dough is achieved. (Optional)

Using a 6" spring structure container, spread the outside combination in the lower half and search uniformly and thoroughly. With the smooth lower part of a drinking glass, you can get it exceptionally level and even.

Using an electric mixer, blend all of the cheesecake base ingredients until completely smooth and creamy. A cake hitter should be visible in the background. The use of an alter may be necessary if your blender is equipped with such a feature.

Fill the spring structure pan halfway with the player.

Blend all of the ingredients for the raspberry sauce until smooth. Either blend the sauce into the cheesecake player or spoon it on top of the plain cheesecake after it has set, depending on your preference.

6. You may want to defrost it for a couple of hours before serving it.

Place additional raspberries and a light dusting of cinnamon on the plate and serve right away!

Notes

Ideally, cashews should be soaked for 4-6 hours before using them in any recipe. Phytic corrosive substances are diminished, making them more absorbable, and the finished cheesecake has a smooth and velvety surface as a result of this. I am unable to guarantee anything.

that the surface will look very similar if you don't splash the nuts!

Orange cranberry glaze adorns the top of this raw vegan fermented cranberry cheesecake.

Due to the use of aged nut cheddar, this unappealing cake not only resembles a cheesecake, but is also one. DUH! Cheesecake-like in flavor and texture! Yay. Crust is made from the following ingredients:

Pecans, 2 cup

the addition of ten dates

Vanilla extract or the seeds of a vanilla bean (optional) 1 teaspoon vanilla concentrate

cheddar with cashew cream that has been refined

Date glue (about 3/4 cup)

Celtic ocean salt (1/2 teaspoon)

2 teaspoons natural vanilla extract or the seeds from a vanilla bean (optional)

coconut butter (half a cup)

Instructions

Blend the ingredients listed above until they are smooth and creamy (about 30 seconds).

Add a handful of dried cranberries and mix thoroughly.

1/3 of the filling should be set aside, and the remaining 3/4 cup cranberries should be mixed in for the top layer, which should be decorated with walnuts and a cranberry glaze made with 1/2 cup date syrup.

affixing 1/4 cup orange juice and some orange rind, 1/4 cup coconut oil, 3/4 cup cranberries, and 1 teaspoon vanilla extract blended until smooth, then add in whole cranberries; blend again.

Make a sauce to go with the cake to make it more festive.

Pie made with sweet potatoes and pecans.

Time required for preparation: 10 minutes || Time required for total completion: 10 minutes Vegan Dishes Are Available 8

CPSIA information can be obtained
at www.ICGtesting.com
Printed in the USA
BVHW061040140622
639736BV00008B/404